THE RIGHT TO RECOVER

PERSONAL INJURY - THE RECOVERY YOU DESERVE

Jacquelyn Hughes

Jacobs & Whitehall
73-03 Bell Blvd, #10
Oakland Gardens, NY 11364
www.jacobsandwhitehall.com

Ordering Information:

Quantity sales. Special discounts are available on quantity purchases by corporations, associations, and others. For details, contact the publisher at the address above.

Orders by U.S. trade bookstores and wholesalers. Please contact Jacobs & Whitehall: Tel: (888) 991-2766 or visit www.jacobsandwhitehall.com.

Printed in the United States of America

Published in 2022

ISBN: 978-1-951149-70-3

Preface

The title "The Right to Recover" was born out of my own personal journey towards a healthy lifestyle after experiencing a life-altering accident, as well as numerous discussions I've had over the last several years about what I do as a personal injury attorney and why I think personal injury law is so important. In a legal sense, if you've been injured and someone else is at fault, you have the right to recover an amount of money that will put you in the position you'd be in if the accident never happened.

I believe recovery represents much more than a settlement check. It represents the process you go through to get your life back after something terrible happens. Recovery encompasses taking the steps necessary to regain your physical health and strength. Recovery encompasses finding a way to emotionally move past the negative emotions that come from getting hurt by something totally out of your control. Recovery encompasses getting you back on track financially.

ACKNOWLEDGEMENTS

I am thankful for my family and friends who have supported me, not only in starting my own firm, but who have also celebrated my accomplishments as my firm grows.

I'm grateful for the mentors and colleagues who've taken the time to teach me countless things I need to know but never learned in law school and the colleagues who round-table ideas on case development and strategy.

I'm grateful for the myriad of medical providers who hang in there with me, looking for answers and patiently helping me get stronger, slow though that progress seems, after my own interstate rollover.

DISCLAIMER

This book is intended to be used for educational purposes only. No legal advice is being given, and no attorney-client relationship is intended to be created by reading this book. The author assumes no liability for any errors or omissions or for how this book or its contents are used or interpreted, or for any consequences resulting directly or indirectly from the use of this book. For legal or any other advice, please consult an experienced attorney or the appropriate expert, who is aware of the specific facts of your case and is knowledgeable in the law in your jurisdiction.

HUGHES LAW, PLLC

1690 Rimrock Rd. Ste. F.
Billings, MT 59102
406-855-4979
www.hugheslawmt.com

Testimonials

"Thank you for fighting so hard for us. Thank you for giving us a chance to start moving forward in a positive way. We are both feeling better. I lost 15 lbs.! What I mean to say is that you have given us the chance to breath freely again, where our focus can be on our family, etc., and not always have to pretend that we are okay. Thank you for never giving up and for enduring all that you did. At most times, we were on the sidelines just trying to breathe while you were fighting the battle. Please know, we will never forget and we hope the closing of our case also gives a sigh of relief and great satisfaction that it was only because of you that we finally found the light at the end of the tunnel. Thank you for your great talent, perseverance, fighting spirit, and kindness. We feel blessed and forever grateful."

– C.M. and T.M.

****

"I had an extremely good experience working with Jacqui and her staff to resolve a complicated litigation case. Jacqui was very responsive and answered all my questions quickly and clearly. I have worked with a lot of lawyers and I can say that her ability to get right to the heart of the issue is unparalleled. I could tell that she had the client's best interests at heart and was working tirelessly to resolve this case. I would definitely hire Jacqui again in the future."

– S. M.

****

"Jacqui is an amazing woman and an excellent attorney she helped me with a case that could have ended badly if I hadn't turned to her for help. She kept me informed of everything going on so that I wasn't in the dark and when trial came she was incredible. I definitely couldn't have done that without her and her staff!"

– S. G.

****

Table Of Contents

About The Author

Eight years ago, I was involved in an interstate rollover. It happened so fast and yet I remember it in slow motion. Realizing the car was out of control. Screaming at the top of my lungs. Turning around mid-rollover, because in the chaos I was terrified my son's car seat wasn't holding. That vivid memory was followed by weeks of mental fog and constant physical pain. Weeks turned into years. I think it was the first time I really understood how hard it is to actually recover; how much pressure there was to work when I really needed time off and how getting better takes more than just time. It takes effort. It takes money. It takes hard work.

If given the choice, I would choose to never have had the experience of waiting in a barrow pit for emergency responders, but the experience gave me an entirely different perspective on how injuries can affect someone's life. I was the primary bread winner for my family. My husband and I had relatively new start up businesses and my son was ten months old. Our health insurance was barely existent and didn't cover the injuries from the accident. My medical providers didn't originally connect my constant pain to the accident and I spent over five years looking for answers before I was finally referred to Mayo Clinic. Over five years after our accident, I finally got answers I could use to begin recovering.

I've personally experienced trying to fit medical care into my budget when there is no room in the budget. I've personally experienced the constant balancing between needing money from working and needing time off to get better. I've experienced the feeling of futility when what was "supposed to work" didn't and no one knew why. A significant amount of my medical bills went to collections. Other bills found their way into a credit card balance I dreaded. I needed time to recover, but I didn't think my family could afford it.

This experience fortified my primary goal in practicing this type of law, which is to help my clients heal. I want to see people recover from their injuries and move forward with their lives. When I say "do what your medical providers tell you to do", it's not because I think that advice is easy to follow; it's because I live the importance of it every single day. When I say "keep trying" it's because I believe there is hope.

What I Want Readers To Gain From This Book:

My goal in writing this book is to provide readers with a basic understanding of what personal injury law is and how it helps with the journey from injury to recovery. I also want readers to know above all else, they should make sure to take care of themselves after an accident. Take the time you need to get better. Take the time you need to make it to physical therapy appointments. Do the exercises, even when it hurts. No amount of compensation will be enough if you don't do everything you can to heal from an injury.

CHAPTER 1

THINGS TO CONSIDER BEFORE AN INJURY

What's best for your life is best for you, so what's best for your life is best for your case. Your goal after an accident is to get your life back on track with minimal interference. With that in mind, the three main things you should do *before* an accident are 1) build the life you want, 2) establish care with a primary care physician, 3) evaluate your own insurance needs.

1. **Build the life you want.**

Live. Really. Really LIVE. Recovering from an accident isn't easy. It's work. It is worthwhile, but it is hard work. A lot of legal words explain the types of compensation you can get or the type of damages you can claim.

The bottom line is "compensation" means you get an amount that puts you in the exact same spot you would be in had the accident never occurred.

The hardest cases I've seen in my career as a personal injury attorney are the cases where someone hated everything about the life he had before an accident and wanted a settlement that would build a different, better life than what he had pre-injury. The harsh reality is the law provides compensation for the life you have. It doesn't compensate you for the life you wish you had.

If you hate every waking moment of your life, figure out why and do whatever you need to do to fix it. If you can't find any value in your employment and you dread going to work, figure out what you want to do and start working your way towards actually doing it. If you feel like your work life and personal life are out of balance, rebalance. Shift your focus from everything that is going wrong to everything that is going right. If it gets to be ten o'clock in the morning and you can't think of three wonderful things you love about today, create some wonderful things to love. If you are lonely, take steps to ease someone else's loneliness and, in doing so, take satisfaction that in easing another's loneliness, you alleviate your own. If you wish you spent more time playing and less time working, find a way to play. Not tomorrow. Not next summer. Not when school starts. Not on January 1 of next year. Change takes time. The sooner you start, the sooner you will see the benefit. Live like there is a possibility that this life on earth is heaven and you can't run the risk of missing it.

If you build the life you want and you don't get into an accident – CONGRATULATIONS – you are living the life you want! If you build the life you want and you do get hurt, you have a life that motivates you to get back to your pre-injury self. You have friends and family to encourage you that pain isn't forever. You have a flicker of passion for your employment motivating you to get back to it. When physical therapy hurts, you will have more determination to slug through it because you know that the physical therapist is pushing you so that you can do the things you love. If you train your mind to focus on the beauty around you, you will have spent time bettering your life and building the skills you will need to recover. The right to recover is yours. The choices that lead to recovery are yours as well. Build the life you want.

2. **Establish care with a primary care physician.**

What's best for your life is best for your case. A dear friend of mine, who is one of the most compassionate and thorough medical providers I know, says the reasons to establish care with a primary care provider are simple and offered the following four points:

A. Preventative care is key to helping you stay healthy. Your primary care provider assists with your health through exams, tests, education, and referrals if needed.

B. You need to have a trusting relationship with your provider. Primary care providers become one of many people's trusted advisors. Having a primary care provider who knows you physically and mentally can help you through the ups and downs of life.

C. Primary care providers are busy. Medical care is a hurry up and wait game. Having someone you can call in an emergency who knows you and your needs is going to benefit you. Whether you need to be seen acutely for an accident or for a long-term problem, when you have a trusted provider you can call, it will reduce the stress of your situation and get you the medical care you need in a much more timely manner.

D. If you do have a tragic event in your life, an established primary care provider would know you before and after the accident. They would be able to attest to your health physically and mentally and help you navigate the treatment you'll need after an event.

You are in the best position possible to recover after an accident when you have the best medical care you can get. You are in the best position to get the best medical care you can get when your provider knows your medical history, knows you aren't faking an injury to obtain prescription pain medication, trusts you to take her advice and knows that you'll follow through on referrals. Find a primary care physician you trust.

3. Evaluate your own insurance needs.

In my practice, I take cases where I believe there is a way to get you compensated, either through insurance or through the assets of the person or entity that injured you. That doesn't always work out the way we want it to. Sometimes, people get hurt and no one is at fault. Sometimes people get hurt and are at fault for their own injuries. Sometimes people get hurt and it is someone else's fault but that person has no ability to pay for the loss.

Regardless of who is paying, you need to get treatment to get your life back on track. You can ensure this process is smoother by knowing you have insurance to at least help with your bills. When you have your own insurance, your mind isn't trying to balance between how much care you need and whether you can afford it. When you have your own insurance, the fact that you are insured will alleviate a lot of the stress associated with unpaid bills. A lower stress level allows your body to heal.

When you have your own insurance, you are less encumbered by what you should have done because you can make decisions without wondering if the treatment will bankrupt you. When my accident happened, we didn't have great health insurance but we had medical payments insurance on our vehicles. Three ambulances, two sheriffs and a highway patrol responded to our accident. We were at least a half hour's ambulance ride to the nearest hospital. The emergency responders unanimously recommended that my ten-month-old be transported by ambulance to the emergency room for a full work up. One responder reassured me that it appeared my son was unharmed but emphasized a baby can't say if he was hit in the head or if something hurts. She gently explained that injuries often aren't immediately visible in accidents as severe as ours. I didn't have to make that decision based on whether I could afford the ambulance and emergency room care because I knew our insurance that would cover it. I can't tell you off the top of my head how much that insurance cost per month. I can tell you every dime was worth it.

When I say evaluate your own insurance needs that includes meeting with an agent who can explain different types of insurance to you, what they are, when they apply, and help you figure out how much you need. There are countless types of insurance out there and what each person needs is different. You are in no better position having the wrong insurance than you are having no insurance. An insurer's website can sell you a policy, but you are far more likely to get what you really need if you sit down with a competent agent you trust who can explain what is out there and if what you have is best for you. Find someone you trust and get the insurance you need so you can get the treatment you need.

CHAPTER 2

FIRST STEPS TO TAKE AFTER AN INJURY

The first two things to do after an accident or injury are to report the accident to the proper people and to get medical care. The order in which to do these two things depends on how severe your injuries are. If your injuries are life threatening, seek medical help first. If you don't need immediate medical assistance, stay at the scene and make sure the accident is properly reported. Then get medical care. Once those two things are taken care of, notify your employer and others who need to know about your accident, put the insurer on notice and, if necessary, file a lawsuit.

1. Report the accident:

If you were in an auto accident, call law enforcement and wait for the police to arrive. This isn't just a good idea – it is something you're legally required to do, and, in Montana, there are fines associated with leaving the scene.

There is no limitation on where an accident or injury can occur. Homes, stores, recreational complexes, your place of work… Notify the owner or employer of the injury. If it is a work-related injury, follow the process for reporting a work-related injury to your employer and to the Department of Labor.

Many places have procedures in place to document the injury and the condition that caused the injury. If you don't tell anyone there was an accident, they have no way to know they need to document the accident, injury, or condition that caused the injury. A lot of the information needed to establish liability comes from the first few hours after the accident. Various pieces of evidence like names and contact information of witnesses, pictures of the scene, or video surveillance are often available but aren't gathered or kept if no one knows there was an injury. Down the road, you will be putting your efforts into physical healing, while I will be putting my efforts into evaluating whether someone is responsible for your injury. If you don't report the injury, the evidence I need to establish liability can be lost.

If you are in a place where it is safe to do so and your medical condition doesn't require emergency care, take some pictures of the scene. More likely than not, you've seen episodes of legal shows on television where an attorney masterfully recreates an accident scene and the reconstruction is so compelling there couldn't possibly be a chance of losing the case. Attorneys do make use of accident reconstruction, but there is no reconstruction as powerful as the actual accident scene. It can be uncomfortable to ask people who saw the accident for their name and telephone number, but often those people are willing to help. Your recollection of the accident is crucial, and when it comes to proving a dangerous condition existed, the more people that saw it, the stronger your case will be. You can't assume someone else will get the names and telephone numbers of witnesses to the accident. I've had numerous cases where my client insists there were people at the accident scene who waited to talk with law enforcement… But when I get the police report, no witnesses are listed. The witness testimony of uninvolved bystanders is often what makes or breaks your case. It's awkward to ask for a name and contact information at an accident scene, especially if you think someone else should be doing it. If you count on someone else to do it, it might not get done and that isn't a risk you want to take if you can avoid it.

Auto accidents are probably the easiest example I can use to explain the importance of making sure the proper people are notified. As a fifteen-year-old with a learner's permit, my dad routinely emphasized (and by routinely, I mean every time we were in a car together) you *never* allow the other person to leave the scene of an accident. By "emphasized" I mean it was pretty clear I wouldn't lose the car if I was in an accident, but if I failed to report it, my wheels wouldn't leave the driveway. His supporting anecdotal statement was always the same. Decades before I even knew what driving was, my grandma was traveling south when a driver traveling north crossed a double yellow line, came into my grandmother's lane, side-swiped her, and forced her off the road. The driver of the other vehicle stopped, acknowledged she was at fault, claimed she was running late and hadn't been paying attention. She was quite frantic about an appointment she would miss if they waited for law enforcement to arrive, so my grandma agreed she could leave and they would work with the insurance companies later. When "later" came, the story changed dramatically - she claimed my grandmother was at fault and there were no other witnesses to the scene. Needless to say, the other driver didn't pay for the damage to my grandmother's car. While trying to be kind, my grandma unwittingly ended up financially responsible for an accident that wasn't her fault.

People generally aren't the most trustworthy versions of themselves when they realize they might be responsible for someone else's injury. People will leave the scene of an accident. People will clean up a dangerous condition. People will make repairs of conditions they'd previously ignored. People will change their story. The best-intentioned person will often forget important details, even when they want to help.

Put the responsible person on notice. Ask for the name and contact information of their insurance carrier. Get the names and contact information of the people who saw the accident. Take pictures.

2. Get Medical Care

Get medical care and start the process of getting the treatment you need. Medical care is expensive. Medical care is time consuming. Sometimes it is difficult to find a doctor that will take on primary care of someone who is in litigation or potentially headed towards litigation. I understand there are hurdles and what you are going through isn't easy. But when it comes to pursuing recovery for your injuries, I can't help you financially if you don't find someone to help you medically.

Throughout the course of your case, you'll encounter a lot of people making judgments, good and bad, about you and your approach to your injuries. You and your case will be reviewed by medical providers, insurance adjusters, defense attorneys, mediators, judges, and possibly jurors. Regardless of whether the assumption is accurate, most of these people believe if your injury is real and your pain is real, you will have gotten medical attention. Most people strongly believe that people who are in pain will do whatever they can to get out of pain.

3. Notify your employer and others.

Notify your employer if you are going to miss work. Be aware of others that depend on you and notify them if you aren't able to follow through on something. Your friends and family will most likely be understanding and want to help you – let them!

4. Put the insurance company on notice.

If you know who the insurance carrier is, contact it and open a claim. They will ask for a statement, and you need to provide one so the insurer can investigate your claim. The insurer will make a determination as to whether it is responsible to cover your losses, and, if it is, will make arrangements for you to submit medical bills and lost wage claims. You aren't stuck with an insurer's determination that it isn't responsible for your losses. If they deny your claim, find out what their appeal process is or contact an attorney to evaluate liability.

5. If necessary, file a lawsuit.

I often face the question: How long can I wait before filing a personal injury claim after being injured in Montana? The length of time a person can wait before filing a lawsuit is known as the statute of limitations. If you have a claim and the lawsuit isn't filed with the court by the end of the statute of limitations, you can't pursue the claim.

How long you have to file the claim depends on the type of claim and the theory of liability. In Montana, the statutes of limitations I most commonly deal with, range between six months and ten years. This is a huge range, and I can't tell you how long the statute applicable to your case is without knowing what type of case you have.

It is important to understand that waiting until the last minute to address your injury is horrible for your case. Depending upon the type of claim you have, the initial investigation and evaluation can take six months to a year. No attorney wants to be filing a lawsuit and figuring out as she goes whether she sued the right defendant and if the defendant she sued is, in fact, the at-fault party. No attorney wants to learn a year into a lawsuit that there is no insurance and the defendant has no assets.

Waiting until the last minute to look for legal help is also horrible for your case because it significantly impairs my ability to prove that your injuries are related to the accident and that the other party was at fault. What I can recover for you is directly connected to the injury you have, your diagnosis, your efforts to recover, and the ability to prove your losses resulted from the accident.

If you wait three years to look into whether you have a case, crucial pieces of your case are lost and critical time for injury healing has passed. In most of my cases, treating physicians will advocate for my client (who is their patient). Treating physicians most often won't provide an opinion that a certain injury resulted from an accident if the patient doesn't seek treatment until two years after the accident. This isn't because your doctor is heartless, uncaring, and unreasonable; it is because he can't tell two years after the accident whether your injury was related to the accident or caused by an incident that occurred at some point in the two years between the accident and when you sought treatment.

Waiting to pursue a case also impairs your ability to physically recover. I am not a doctor, but I have had many medical providers explain to me that the healing process immediately after the injury is much faster and as time goes on, the healing process slows. If you wait too long to get medical treatment, your injuries change from acute (and more likely to be temporary) to chronic (and more likely to be permanent). The chances of fully recovering decline over time. What it takes to recover from an injury isn't always intuitive and, without proper medical care, you can end up developing habits that make your injuries worse.

For example, it isn't uncommon in cases involving back injuries for a person to decrease activity hoping the pain will go away. Muscles that support the spine start to weaken. Other muscles become tense and tight to compensate for the weakness. It is a vicious cycle of avoiding pain, decreasing activity, experiencing an increase in pain, attempting to avoid the pain by further decreasing activity, and so on. When you finally decide that reduced activity isn't working, the course of physical therapy can be slower, longer, more painful, and less successful long-term.

Due to delaying treatment, you are in a worse position starting physical therapy six months after the accident than if you had started right away.

The primary goal of my legal practice is to get you the compensation you need to get back to who you were and what you had before you were injured. If you wait to pursue your rights, your ability to recover physically and my ability to obtain financial recovery are both impaired.

For this reason, it is best to consult with an attorney about your case, what you should do, and the statutes of limitations that apply. This is true even if getting the compensation you deserve doesn't necessarily require an attorney. Not every accident requires an attorney's assistance to get the compensation you deserve. Some insurance companies will do the right thing, will process your medical bills on time, and send compensation for lost wages as lost wages are incurred. In cases where the insurance company or at-fault party are doing what they should do, you may not need an attorney. However, it is always wise to speak with an attorney to make sure you are doing what you need to be doing, the at-fault party is doing what s/he needs to be doing and should the insurer or at-fault party's conduct become problematic, you have done what you need to preserve your claim.

CHAPTER 3

FACTORS THAT DETERMINE VIABILITY OF A PERSONAL INJURY CASE

There are numerous considerations that determine whether it is viable to pursue any given case. Some of these factors are the credibility of the injured party, establishing the liability of the at-fault party, nature and severity of your injuries in relation to how much it will cost to pursue a claim, and insurance coverage or other financial assets.

1. Credibility of the Injured Party

It is absolutely critical my clients are honest. Honest when they give a statement. Honest with their medical providers. Honest with their friends and family. Honest with me. No case is perfect. No person is perfect. I can deal with imperfections, but I can't deal with imperfections about which I don't know, and I won't put my reputation on the line to pursue a case for a client I can't trust. Be honest. Sometimes that may mean you don't have a case. It is far better to learn that you don't have a case early than to put your time into a losing case.

2. Liability of the At-Fault Party

I can't pursue a case if I can't establish liability. Liability is the fancy word for "at fault". If the person or entity that injured you didn't do anything wrong, they aren't responsible for compensating you for your injuries. I have had potential clients call me, absolutely convinced the property owner is responsible just because an injury happened on their property. If the potential client overloaded the trunk of his car and fell, striking his head while trying to force the trunk closed, it doesn't matter that the injury happened on someone else's property. There is no at fault party other than the injured person, and that means no recovery.

Establishing liability often requires investigation and research. By no means is it always clear who is at fault for an injury, or whether anyone is at fault. Proving liability involves being able to explain what the person did wrong and how that differs from what a reasonable person would have done. The standard isn't perfection; it is whether the potentially at fault person acted as a reasonable person.

I regularly see cases where liability is strong in one area but it is cost-prohibitive to pursue, as the financial benefit to my client is outweighed by the cost of pursuing the claim. If it costs more to pursue a claim than you will recover, it isn't worth pursuing.

However, there are often not-so-obvious but far less costly avenues of recovery, and finding these avenues is one thing I love about practicing law. If, for some reason, the obvious path to liability doesn't work, it is often well worth the time to research less obvious paths.

3. Nature and severity of injuries in relation to the cost of recovery

Evaluating the nature and severity of injuries as they relate to the costs involved in recovery requires looking very closely at the costs that will be put into your case, and whether at the end of the case, I will be able to recover enough money to make the case worth your time. Potential clients are often offended when I say a case isn't financially viable, as they perceive it to mean I don't care about their particular injury or the wrong inflicted on them. That isn't accurate. What it means when I say a case isn't financially viable is I don't want to drag a client through litigation, compounding the emotional stress of what they've gone through, knowing the costs of pursuing the claim will be higher than the value of the claim itself. There are more costs involved in pursuing a case than just my fee. Your medical providers will charge me to get copies of your records. Depending on how far the case goes, I will need to interview witnesses under oath (depositions). The transcripts for a deposition range between five hundred and a few thousand dollars. If I need to depose your medical providers, I will have to advance the costs to compensate the doctors for their time, often in excess of $2,000.00. If someone comes to me with a relatively minor dog bite with a few stitches and an emergency room bill of $1,500.00, I know the costs of pursuing the claim, plus my fee, far exceed the value of the case and my client won't see a benefit from the litigation. I won't pursue a claim "on principle" if it won't benefit my client. For a case to be viable, there has to be a financial benefit to my client. If the costs exceed the recovery, it isn't financially viable.

4. Insurance and Other Assets.

The at-fault party must either be insured or have assets that can be used to compensate you or the case isn't viable. If I obtain a multi-million-dollar verdict against someone who is bankrupt, my client has nothing more than a piece of paper with big numbers on it. You can't squeeze blood out of a turnip. It doesn't matter how much the case is worth if the at fault party has no money to pay the judgment.

CHAPTER 4

INFORMATION TO SHARE WITH YOUR ATTORNEY

What information should an injured person share with their personal injury attorney? All of it. Answer my questions. Every question. Don't try to anticipate what information I'm trying to get or how it will be used. Give me more information than you think I could ever need. Bring me every piece of paper you think might be related to the case and if I don't need it, I'll give it back to you. The more details a client shares with me, the better equipped I am to figure out who is responsible, how severe the injury is, what theories of liability are viable, and if there are assets or insurance coverage available to compensate you for the injuries. It also helps me figure out what compensation you deserve. My goal is to get you the money you need to get back to who you would be if the accident hadn't happened. To do that, I need to know a lot about you.

Lawsuits are like puzzles where the pieces come in different boxes and, even when all of the boxes are collected, there are still a few pieces missing. I need enough puzzle pieces for the complete picture to be identifiable. The majority of the puzzle pieces come from you either giving me the puzzle pieces or giving me enough information to find the puzzle pieces. Some puzzle pieces come from your medical records. Some puzzle pieces come from the accident report. Some puzzle pieces come from pictures. Some from witness statements. Some from experts. Some from your employer. Some from our opponent. The more pieces of the puzzle I have, the clearer the picture of liability, injury, loss, and recovery. If there are big portions of the puzzle missing, the other side will argue it is because the picture we are trying to present doesn't exist. I need as many puzzle pieces as we can find. Tell me everything you can remember about the accident, about your treatment, about your recovery.

This is important not only because, as time goes on, memories often fade or change but because trauma can alter even the most vivid memories. Trauma rewires our brains in ways science is barely beginning to understand. In all likelihood, you will forget some things. Time will change how you remember others. Some details will be vivid and unforgettable. Other details will be blurred, as though you were there... but not really. If there is a puzzle piece that doesn't fit, I need to know so I can figure out why it doesn't fit and how to address it.

Tell me who your medical providers are. All of them. Even if you don't think they're related. I need to be able to evaluate the full picture. Generally, my clients are honest with me, but there are people who aren't. Early in my career, I defended against a claim where the person claiming my client injured her had sued another person for the exact same injury a few years prior. Had she been honest about the injury, an argument could have been made that the injury was worsened by the second accident. As she had completely covered it up, not disclosed it to her attorney and lied about it, under oath, her credibility was shot - and so was her case. I can work with imperfections; credibility issues are infinitely harder.

As your case goes on, I will ask a lot of questions. Everything you tell me is privileged, which means that nobody can make me disclose our discussions. Injuries, the effects they have on our lives, medical treatment, and the physical and emotional battles we face are intensely personal. The truth about what your life was like before an injury and how the injury changed your life isn't ever pretty. For most of my clients, it isn't easy to talk about the way an injury has impacted their life. Hard conversations are hard. They are also necessary. No matter how uncomfortable it is, it is crucial to your case that you share the information with me.

Chapter 5

Common Mistakes Clients Make

Every case is unique. Every client's injuries are unique. Every client's employment situation is unique. The numerous factors that go into what a case is worth make it difficult to give blanket advice on what might weaken a case. That said, there are a few things I've seen over the years that, without fail, will weaken my client's case:

1) Not being clear with medical providers about the nature of the accident and physical condition;
2) Downplaying injuries (or exaggerating them);
3) Not following through with your medical provider's recommendations;
4) Discussing your case on social media;
5) Expecting your case to resolve quickly; and
6) Focusing more on your case than your physical recovery.

1. **Be clear with medical providers about the nature of the accident and physical condition;**

You need to have a medical provider you trust, and you need to be completely honest with your medical provider about what hurts and how bad it hurts. Your medical providers make their decisions based on the information you give them. If you don't tell them you're having headaches, they won't look for headaches or provide treatment for headaches. Your providers can't treat conditions about which they don't know! They can't document conditions about which they don't know. And they can't testify about conditions unless they know about them.

If a client comes to me after an accident and wants compensation for a debilitating back injury but there isn't a single mention of back pain in two years of medical records, it's going to be extremely difficult, if not impossible, to show that the back pain is related to the accident. Sitting in an exam room after an accident and trying to list everything that hurts is mentally taxing, especially in the first few weeks when your physical condition seems to be constantly changing. We are in a much better position if you tell your doctor about all of your injuries than we are trying to explain, "I've had headaches all along, but I was too nauseated to tell my doctor."

Being clear with your providers about what hurts and how bad it hurts helps you get the treatment you need to recover physically and emotionally. It gives me the paper trail and witnesses I need to be able to show how severe your injuries are and how they've impacted your life.

Along those lines, be sure your doctor is noting what you tell them. If we get medical records and you don't think they are correct, we can submit a request to correct the record. Be transparent with your medical providers. Get the help you need to recover.

2. Don't downplay your injuries (or exaggerate them).

It's common to want to reassure family and friends that you are okay and that things are "fine." This doesn't help anyone if you aren't truly okay. Downplaying your injuries often results in not getting the treatment you need and not following restrictions that will help you get better. It also results in presenting an image to the people closest to you that you aren't hurt; an image that is inconsistent with what you are really going through. Be real about your injuries and be real about the affects they are having on your life.

The opposite of downplaying your injuries is a problem as well. Don't exaggerate your injuries. If you rate a paper cut at a ten on the scale of zero to ten, ten being the worst pain imaginable, it isn't credible. Be real about your injuries and be real about the affects they are having on your life. (Yes – I said it twice – it's that important!)

3. Follow through with your medical provider's recommendations

Not following through with your provider's advice creates countless problems with your case. I won't describe them all, but the lesson is this:

Do what your medical provider tells you to do. If you don't trust his or her advice, find a medical provider you trust and do what s/he tells you to do.

First, your case is about your healing. If you are not putting the effort into healing, you are hurting your life and you are hurting your case. A lot of injury treatment is uncomfortable and sometimes even painful. Physical therapy hurts. Chiropractic care hurts. Surgeries hurt. The goal is that by going through the steps to get better, even though they cause additional pain in the short term, in the long term your injuries will heal. The treatment may be painful, uncomfortable, and exhausting, but it is worth it in the long term because the treatment helps your injuries heal and, theoretically, you will experience less pain for a shorter period of time.

If you follow your medical provider's recommendations and the injuries don't heal, we can argue you've done everything you can to get better and it's not working. If you don't follow your medical provider's recommendations, a jury will question whether you were hurt that badly to begin with and whether your injuries are permanent because of the accident or permanent because you wouldn't put the effort into getting better.

Following your medical provider's treatment recommendations goes beyond just the treatment you are receiving. If your medical provider sets activity restrictions for you, follow them. Yes, it's inconvenient to be limited to lifting ten pounds for a few months, but it's much more inconvenient to experience your injury worsening instead of getting better because you were too proud to ask someone to carry your laundry basket.

If your medical provider recommends certain types of testing, get the testing. I've had clients with back pain radiating into their feet tell me they won't participate in a nerve conduction study because it hurts, or they won't go through with an MRI because it feels claustrophobic. If those are really the reasons deterring you from testing, talk with your medical provider about another alternative testing, or ways to cope with the pain or fear. If you deny your medical provider the ability to investigate the cause of your injury, he isn't going to be able to tell me what the injury is, what caused it, and why it is affecting you the way it is.

Following your medical provider's recommendations with respect to time off work or returning to work is crucial as well. If your medical provider says rest, then rest. If your medical provider says you can return to work, return to work. If you think you aren't ready to return to work, get a second opinion. If you return to work and your pain worsens, go back and revisit the issue with your medical provider.

Follow through with your medical provider's recommendations. It's what you need to do to get better, and it's what I need from you to make your case strong.

4. **Don't discuss your case on social media. For that matter, temporarily take a break from social media while you are recovering.**

Don't discuss your case on social media. Actually, don't be on social media. Social media is a virtual reality where most people are posting based on how they want other people to see them. It's an image we create for our "friends." An image is created with every post regardless of whether you are trying to create one. An inaccurate image can be used to discredit you. An announcement to your friends and family of your first pain free day after the injury can be used by your opponent to argue that you were fully recovered as of that day. There is no way social media will benefit your case. If you post every day and never mention your accident or injury, the defense will argue that it wasn't that significant to you. If you post every day and discuss your pain in detail, any inconsistency will be compared to your medical records and used to create credibility problems. If your pain is the only thing you post about, it will look like you are hanging onto the pain instead of trying to get better. There is no winning in social media. Don't post. Use the time to take a break from social media. If you have posted, don't delete it, but stop posting.

5. **Don't expect your case to resolve quickly.**

I had a marketing agent a few years repeatedly tell me I needed to advertise "swift legal action" and "quick recoveries." "Swift legal action" is a fiction. "Quick recoveries" aren't a reality. Investigating your case takes time. Your recovery will likely take time.

One of my very first clients became incredibly angry with me because she believed her case could be resolved in six weeks, and from what she relayed to me, was told by another attorney (who didn't take her case) that it should resolve…within six weeks. I can't get a full set of medical records and bills in six weeks, let alone any follow up the information needed to fully evaluate the case. I can't move the case forward without evaluating it. Physical recovery isn't quick. Recovering financially isn't quick.

Legal-related television shows are interesting, but I've yet to see one that doesn't create expectations that I could file a lawsuit tomorrow and go to trial at the beginning of next week. This isn't the reality for anyone, anywhere, no matter how amazing their attorney is. In cases that go to trial, the first trial setting is usually at least a year out.

I don't get paid until you get paid, so believe me when I say, "I want your case to move quickly." You also need to believe me when I say that litigation isn't easy or fast.

6. **Don't get distracted from the healing process by focusing on your settlement.**

It is very easy for clients to become preoccupied with the ultimate settlement amount, but this often precludes them from focusing on their own health and recovery. Some clients will become so preoccupied with recovering financially that they will be counting on a certain amount of money at a very specific time, which doesn't give me the opportunity to maximize their case. It also robs them of the ability to fully recover. It creates an expectation about the financial recovery that is in no way related to their actual losses.

If people are trying to get better, it shows; if people are focused only on the settlement, it shows. If someone has put their efforts into getting better and has been following all of the doctor's recommendations, then they will present to the jurors in a more likable light than someone who has put all of their efforts into a preoccupation with the settlement amount.

Having been through a pretty catastrophic injury myself, I understand how hard it can be to not worry about money and the expense of the injury. However, when people focus on how they can afford to get better, they cut corners on treatment and prolong their injuries indefinitely. If a client can separate themselves from the costs, they will put themselves in a much better position for healing and moving on with their life.

CHAPTER 6

VALUING YOUR CASE

At almost every initial client meeting, my potential client asks: "What is my case worth?" Inevitably, I answer, "I don't know right now." It's not that I don't understand my client's need for answers or that I don't get that this answer is frustrating; it's that I really can't know at that first meeting what the case might be worth and it isn't helpful to you or your case for me to give a number and later find out I can't make that number materialize into a settlement. There are many, many factors that determine how much your case is worth, some of which you can control and some of which you can't.

How you were injured matters. An accident at 8:00 a.m. caused by a driver with a 0.32 BAC will be worth more than a rear-end accident resulting from black ice. One is an egregious act that a jury will hate. The other is an accident. The injury might be the same in both cases, but how the accident happened matters.

Your type of employment and the impact of your specific injury on your ability to do your job will affect your case. For example, assume the injury is a broken ankle. A client with a broken ankle who does sedentary work and can continue to work will generally receive less compensation than a client with a broken ankle who does manual labor. The injury is the same, but the way it affects the client's ability to earn an income is different because the sedentary work can accommodate a broken ankle and manual labor can't.

In cases involving lost wages, the ability to find work that can accommodate your physical restrictions in your city will play a role. Some of the highest lost wages verdicts in Montana go to railroad employees. This is because they are high wage earners with a very technical skillset, and the skill set to operate a locomotive doesn't transfer easily into other available jobs with comparable pay.

How your medical providers perceive your injuries and your efforts to get better matters. Some medical providers will advocate zealously for their patients. Some won't. Doctors will note in your file if you were referred to physical therapy and didn't follow through. If they tell you that chiropractic care will aggravate your specific type of injury and you go anyway, they will note that. Your medical providers are the foundation to you getting better. Their opinions are the foundation to maximizing your recovery.

Social perceptions matter. Popular beliefs about litigation are constantly changing. Some people believe it is a way to right wrongs. Other people perceive it as a way for litigants to make easy money – the "litigation lottery." All kinds of socio-economic factors affect how compassionate people are towards others' pain and suffering. Juries in some cities will give a high damages award in cases where the same case would result in a defense verdict if tried in a rural community.

Insurance policy limits of the at-fault party or the ability to locate other assets to satisfy a judgment also play a role in assessing case value. For example, if the at-fault party has a $25,000 policy limit and no assets, they will be judgment-proof. It won't matter if the case is worth $30,000 or $3,000,000. The amount I'll be able to recover will be $25,000.

My case evaluation involves looking at the facts of your particular accident, what kind of accident resulted in your injuries, how severely you were injured, how the injuries affected your life, how much money it will take to restore you to the person you were before the accident, researching jury verdicts on similar cases, and comparing how those cases are similar to and different from your case. The value of your case can go up or down with any new piece of information I obtain.

Finally, client credibility will make or break a case. Insurance companies will evaluate a client's credibility. If you aren't credible, their settlement evaluation will be lower. Adjusters will evaluate your ability to sit through the trial. If they figure out my client wouldn't be able to hold it together for a five-day trial, I can expect a lowball offer. If my client doesn't have the attention span, is too hot-headed, or has just lost interest in the litigation process, that will have a negative impact on the case. If my client doesn't care, a jury won't care. Be credible. Be engaged.

CHAPTER 7

IMPORTANCE OF SEEKING TIMELY MEDICAL ATTENTION AFTER SUSTAINING AN INJURY

I can't emphasize enough that the economic recovery I can obtain for you is directly related to your course of physical and emotional recovery after an accident. I also can't emphasize enough that no amount of money will make an injury feel "worth it." The main reason I do what I do is to see people recover. Delays in treatment are delays in recovery— physical, emotional, and financial. Don't delay getting treatment.

I'm not a doctor, but from what I understand the healing process occurs at a much faster rate immediately after the injury. As months or years go on, healing may continue, but at a much slower rate. Most people will gain more from physical therapy early on than they will gain by doing the same exact treatment a year after the accident.

To compound the problem, injury recovery can be counter-intuitive, and if you don't get treatment from someone who knows how to treat your injuries, you could be self-treating your injuries in a way that makes your condition worse. People develop poor body mechanics to avoid experiencing pain. Instead of starting the healing process, the injuries get worse. Muscles weaken. While you are "resting" you may actually be deconditioning. Alternatively, some people think they can just power through the pain. Depending on the injury, "powering through" can send your recovery straight backwards. If you don't know what your injuries are and how to treat them, you could be making them worse.

Clients often find it easier to get help for injuries that can be seen and, psychologically, it is easier to accept that an injury is an injury if you can see it. Someone with an injury like a broken leg will find it easier to get medical help and take necessary time off than someone with an invisible injury like whiplash. While it's easier to appreciate an injury you can see, it's often the unseen injuries that have the most devastating and long-lasting effects. You won't know unless you get treatment.

In addition to the importance of getting treatment so you can start recovery, you need to get treatment so that I have the evidence I need to support your claim. If you wait six months after an accident to visit your medical provider, it will be far more difficult for me to establish that the accident, and not some intervening event, caused your injury. It is far easier to establish causation when you see a medical provider immediately after the accident and follow through on their treatment recommendations.

Chapter 8

Paying For Medical Treatment While Waiting To Resolve Your Case

The Montana Supreme Court has imposed advance pay requirements, which means that insurance companies can't wait until a settlement is final before paying for certain types of costs as those costs are incurred. In other words, liability insurance companies are required to pay medical bills and lost wages as those expenses are incurred, so long as liability for the accident is reasonably clear and it is reasonably clear that the injury being treated is related to the accident. In many cases, the at-fault party's liability insurance information is provided to the medical provider and the liability insurance is billed directly.

Sometimes we ask that the providers submit the records to my client's health insurance company. In some cases, the health insurer will have the ability to request repayment when the case is settled. Despite having to repay what the health insurer paid during the case, it is a good way to see that there are no breaks in treatment that interfere with the healing process. Additionally, your health insurance provider often has contracts with medical providers to pay a reduced amount for certain services. For example, if physical therapy costs $250 an hour and your health insurance company contracted with the provider for $95 an hour, the provider writes off the $155 balance. Often, this means that less of the liability coverage is absorbed by medical expenses than it would be if the bills were paid directly by the liability insurance carrier.

A third way of paying for medical treatment during the pendency of a case is to use medical payments coverage under the client's own automobile medical payments coverage if she has that coverage as part of her insurance.

Where insurance isn't available and the client can't pay for treatment, I will ask that the medical provider put a lien against my file, which means that I will pay them out of any settlement received.

Sometimes, none of the above work, and medical bills go to collections. I wish I wasn't writing that, but it is a harsh reality that some injured people face. For my clients, I advise them to worry less about what is in collections and more about making sure they are better. A bad credit score is often easier to repair, or live with, than a permanent injury that could have been treated.

CHAPTER 9

HOW FUTURE EXPENSES ARE CALCULATED IN PERSONAL INJURY CASES?

Past expenses are easy, right? We can look at what you were making before versus what you made after the accident. Past medical bills have already been charged, so we have exact numbers there. But what about your future expenses? Luckily, we don't need a crystal ball with an exact prediction of what you will need, but we do have to have expert testimony about what you'll need and we have to prove those needs will "more probably than not" occur. Not every case requires an intensive work up on future losses and the strategy isn't the same in every case. That said, there are a few common experts we rely on to help us answer the question of future damages.

The evaluation starts with your medical diagnosis. What are your injuries? What treatment works for you? What treatment doesn't work? How has your recovery progressed? From there, a medical provider can give an opinion on what future medical treatment you are likely to need and what can be expected from that treatment.

We will get opinions on how long your treatment will take, how long your recovery will be, how successful your treatment is likely to be, how much time you will need off work if you will be able to return to work, and how much your medical treatment is expected to cost. That process gives us a pretty accurate reflection of what your future medical costs will be.

We rely on your medical providers to tell us what your work limitations are. If you can't return to work, sometimes we'll hire a vocational rehabilitation specialist to look at your education, skills, and what work you might be able to do.

From there, an economist evaluates what you were making, what it will cost to retrain or obtain an alternate degree, the time it will take to find new employment, and any other factors that might affect your income. The economist will provide his or her calculation of what your future lost wages will be.

Almost everything I do to calculate your losses will stem from what kind of injuries you have. I can't calculate losses for future medical treatment if you don't get treatment.

CHAPTER 10

HOW DO YOU DETERMINE WHETHER TO SETTLE A PERSONAL INJURY CASE OR TAKE IT TO TRIAL?

This is a constantly moving target and involves constantly re-evaluating potential jury verdicts for this case and comparing the potential outcomes to the cost of going to trial. As discussed above, the value of a case is constantly changing, and every one of those changes affects the decision of whether to settle or to keep moving forward through trial.

The benefit of settling is that the risk of a bad jury verdict is gone. The drawback is that a settlement is a compromise, so it is rare that the dollar amount of a settlement will be similar to the dollar amount of the potential verdict. Both parties are buying peace with the finality of a settlement, and the price tag for the peace is what is probably a smaller payout. A factor many people don't understand is that trials are so expensive that a person can often take a smaller settlement and actually end up with more money by avoiding the costs of trial.

Every case has a different amount of costs associated with it. The more medical providers we need to testify, the more costly the trial will be. Experts needed to prove liability will increase the costs of going to trial. If the accident was in a remote location and medical providers or retained experts have to travel long distances to give testimony, that increases the cost of a trial.

Determining whether to take a case to trial depends on how much the case is worth, how much money it is going to take to get the case through trial, how much the case would be worth if we win at trial, the likelihood of winning, and how much the defense is offering.

Sometimes these factors don't change much over time, but they can. If a month before your trial an identical case is tried in front of a jury and the jury awarded nothing for pain and suffering, that will affect the estimated trial value of your case. If the theory of liability is initially weak, but in the months before your trial new science comes out that strengthens liability, your case value will go up. If a key witness changes his or her testimony, that change will affect your case.

Its cliché, but we need to strike when the iron is hot. We need to know the case, both its strengths and weaknesses. We need to know the damages. We need to know recent jury verdicts in similar cases and the underlying factors that created those verdicts. And we need to anticipate what's coming and look for a window of opportunity to settle. If no window of opportunity opens, we take the case to trial.

CHAPTER 11

HOW LONG DOES IT TAKE TO RECEIVE FUNDS AFTER A SETTLEMENT?

The time it takes to receive funds once a settlement amount is agreed upon by all parties varies greatly depending on the case. I've had turnaround times as short as two weeks and as long as eight months. Short turnaround times are more common for cases that I have been working on for a long time because I know exactly what has been paid, where the money needs to go, and how to get the money to the client.

If your medical bills were covered by an ERISA health insurer or Medicare/Medicaid, the health insurer or Medicare/Medicaid may have a legal right to be reimbursed out of the settlement. They have what is called a "lien". If there are ERISA liens or Medicare/Medicaid liens, then I will have to negotiate those prior to giving money to the client. Medicare will usually reduce liens by a third to account for my fees. ERISA is pretty unpredictable; sometimes the insurer will waive the lien altogether, sometimes it won't. If an ERISA company demands the money, then we will evaluate whether they are entitled to get it back under the terms of its insurance plan and work from there.

Typically, health insurers, Medicare, and Medicaid won't negotiate liens until there is a final settlement, and I can't give the client their funds until those liens have been resolved. I am fully aware that this isn't an answer that clients want to hear, but it's an uncertainty that I just can't fix.

I want you to receive your money as quickly as possible, but it could take several months.

Chapter 12

Should You Handle Your Personal Injury Case Without Assistance Of Counsel?

It depends. If your injuries are relatively minor (something all reputable and morally conscious personal injury attorneys hope for), you may be better off handling your claim by yourself. Under such circumstances, you may end up with less in your pocket if you hire an attorney and have to pay attorney's fees.

More likely than not, though, your insurance adjuster will try to convince you to take less than you deserve. If you feel your insurance adjuster isn't treating you fairly or is undervaluing your claim, you should seek the advice of an experienced personal injury attorney.

CHAPTER 13

WHAT SETS HUGHES LAW APART FROM OTHER FIRMS IN HANDLING PERSONAL INJURY CASES?

I am a sucker for movies based on true stories that show determination to conquer adversity. I know nothing about race cars, but I'm on the edge of my seat the entire time I'm watching Ford vs. Ferrari - and I watch it a lot. There is no getting me away from the screen if I've stumbled across Hidden Figures.

I view my cases much the same way. When a potential client sits across the table from me and tells me her story about what happened, I feel compassion because I know the battle that lies ahead. The process will likely feel defeating and infuriating. But day after day, I'm inspired by seeing clients recover. I'm inspired by the determination I see in people as they find the strength to move past something out of their control.

People come to me when they are injured, overwhelmed, frustrated, and unsure how to proceed.

Their physical conditions are uncertain. Their finances are often wrecked. They are emotionally spent. Because I've been there, I can genuinely tell them there is hope. Through my work, I see people find hope and that is what makes me want to come to work.

I often remind clients "it is worth it to do the work." Seeing what my clients overcome is a constant reminder to me that "it is worth it to do the work."

NOTES

Made in the USA
Monee, IL
05 November 2026

67387967R00048